HOW TO AUSTRALIA WITHOUT A WEDDING ORGANISER

And still pull off a fabulous day in fifteen months!

Nicola

LOVE BOOKS

Copyright © 2025 by Nicola Pitt

All rights reserved.

No part of this book may be reproduced in any form or by any electronic or mechanical means, including information storage and retrieval systems, without written permission from the author, except for the use of brief quotations in a book review.

Ebook ISBN: 978-1-922369-76-5

Print ISBN: 978-1-922369-77-2

WHO IS THIS BOOK AIMED AT?

I wrote this after spending months planning my daughter's wedding and hanging around on the wedding groups and boards. I don't know how many brides I saw who said, 'I don't know where to begin' or 'I'm so stressed getting started', so this is for those brides.

A wedding is a day, one of the utmost importance it's true, and yet the stress and worry that comes with trying to plan it all out, especially when most of the guides are American or aimed at brides who are using organisers, cannot be understated. It's hard to know where to begin or even what questions to ask.

But as money gets tighter, more and more brides are looking for ways to do it cheaper, DIY it, or head to locations outside of major cities in search of a cheaper or more purposeful location, they need a strategy for getting to the end. These are the brides look who for a book they can use to step through the essential planning, with an easy to follow guide.

I hope you find this book to be just the thing you need. One last point, is that although this book is aimed at fifteen months, it can be condensed as desired, all you need to do is perhaps combine some of the early months together.

Thank you also to Samantha for reading it through for me ahead of publication.

Good luck and happy planning!

Nicola Pitt

CONTENTS

Just getting started…	1
Month 1: The Venue & Celebrant	5
Month 2: Let's talk about food, cakes & some legal stuff	9
Month 3: Photographers, Videographers, Musicians and more	13
Month 4: Cars, Wedding Party and Flowers	17
Month 5: Starting to get organised… including invitations	21
Month 6: Thinking about the venue layout…	25
Month 7: Take a break and do something fun, next month is the start of the manic period	33
Month 8: Only seven months left!	34
Month 9: Still lots to do	38
Month 10: The downhill run has begun	40
Month 11: We're going to the chapel in a few months…	43
Month 12: Fittings, final instructions and filling out questionnaires	46
Month 13: A last break before it all happens!	48
Month 14: Nearly there!	49
Month 15: The last weeks	52
Your big day arrives	56
What next?	57
Checklists to assist	59
Celebration decorations	61
The music decisions	64
Talky, Talky, Talk… Toasts	65

JUST GETTING STARTED...

There's more things to worry about when planning a wedding than paying more money than you feel is in your budget. This book is my experience of organising weddings (my own and my daughter's) without the benefit of a wedding consultant.

Don't get me wrong, I'm not dissing wedding planners, and some brides want the ease of handing the entire process of putting a wedding together over to someone else. That's perfectly fine, but not everyone has the financial capability or is willing to just give it all up, so here's my quick 'put it together yourself' guide.

Let's start with the basics, okay? He's asked (or she) and you've said yes, but now comes the bit that's daunting. Making the plan and getting the ball started.

Here's my list of what you need in no particular order:

- A celebrant
- Bouquet/s
- Photographer
- Venue
- Wedding Clothes
- Cars (unless you're walking)
- Rings (or other)
- Invitations
- Catering
- Music
- Venue
- Wedding party
- A guest book

For my daughter's recent wedding, we had fifteen months to pull it together and I'll be honest, many of these things are time sensitive. I remember sitting in the lounge and both the bride and groom saying 'but we've got plenty of time.' I may have pointed out then that they really didn't. (At least I had a laid back bride who only got stress-y in the last two months!)

My priority with them was getting the celebrant first. We were lucky, as we knew a couple but this is something you need to book quite early if you have someone in mind, followed by the venue. To be frank, good celebrants book up early.

Where to begin?

I presented the bride and groom with a range of questions.

First, pick the date. Trust me, it sounds like that's further down the line, but it isn't. This is a vital first step in the planning process.

With that chosen, it was who do you want to marry you and where?

Some of these need to be organised ASAP (in bride and groom's place, it was the day he asked and she said yes.) This is vital for arranging the venue, and trust me, you're going to need a short list, We made a couple of phone calls and arranged to go out for a look at what was on the list.

Trust me on this, don't go without a date, because if you love the venue, you can be sure others do too and getting dates is *competitive*. Let me put it like this, at fifteen months out, there were already bookings for the month after bride and groom's chosen date. Don't wait when you're ready to book. Get in and tentatively book your date.

Another thing is I differ from the bridal magazines and books… Don't go looking for inspiration in them, think about what is important to you. I advised daughter to check Pinterest for ideas, dresses, hairstyles etc., that were DIY'able. Why? Because the photos you see in the magazines are perfect, totally set up by photographers, stylists and others. Again, this isn't a bad thing, but if you're doing it yourself you won't necessarily have access to these kinds of set ups, and likely the funds either.

Besides, your wedding is about you. Your vision, what you feel is necessary, achievable and if you're doing it yourself, what you can create.

This is how the journey begins and I'm here to guide you, but at the end of the day, this is your day.

MONTH 1: THE VENUE & CELEBRANT

So you have a date, and a short list of venues. That's the first step. Get online, and find a list of celebrants. Yep, they mostly have Facebook pages and it's my advice you join a couple of local wedding pages/groups too. Why? You'll get feedback on the services near you and that includes both venue and celebrant.

Look at the photos, read what is written, DM and PM people to ask their opinions and feedback. Ring the celebrants and interview them. This is one of the most important days in your life and the person running the ceremony needs to fit you.

Are you a big wedding? Little? Micro? Family only, even. Do you want someone brash or loud, or someone quiet and traditional? Ask how they prepare the ceremony or what advice they give for vows and don't be shy, ask how much they cost too!

Find out how many weddings they've officiated at,

and which ones meant the most. You'll learn a lot there!

Also, if you're choosing a church, be sure to ask what their rules are, do they want a donation or do they charge a set price? When can you set up and if you need to remove items, how soon after?

Often if you're a member of the church, they will assist you with this side of things.

Once you've had a chance to discuss these things, sit down together (bride and groom) and discuss who you felt was the best fit, then get back on that phone and book them. Trust me, good celebrants book up super fast!

Then onto the venue to walk through. Are you having both ceremony and the reception in the same place? How much? What services do they offer? Are they a licensed venue and do they have caterers, photographers etc who they usually work with. (This can be both a blessing and curse, depending on your needs.)

They may have more than one 'location' on site, so check how many weddings will be onsite at the same time, the cost of the venue for the section you want or all of it. In our case, the venue is booked basically from Friday to Sunday for a single price. They do have onsite B&B accomodation and it's not on the beaten path, but offers lush views of the hinterland.

If a discount on accomodation is offered too, check

how many and what the discount is. Quite often you find they book fast or are already fully booked.

In our case, the venue has the cutlery and crockery, tables and chairs along with indoor and outdoor areas, which allow for photographs to be taken onsite. The trade off (which worked excellently for us) was the venue has a maximum size limit with its facilities, for these kinds of events.

Once again, this was a book early situation, and we had to make a deposit within two weeks of booking which I think was in the region of 20% however, the venue should provide you a contract to be signed with all the payment details. In our case, so long as the full payment was made within a certain timeframe you could pay it off.

Do make sure, once you've chosen your venues to go and take photos and ask for measurements, this will make life easier for the planning of decorations later on.

One last step had to be finalised around this point and that was the time of the wedding.

Your venue may need this at the time of booking, so they can make sure they aren't double booked. I recommend this as another early point.

There is one other venue you could consider, and that's your own backyard. And as always, this isn't a bad option either if you're set on saving the money in the kitty.

Pro Tip: Have a back up date if the venue is 'the one' you simply must have in case the date is booked.

JOBS FOR THE FIRST MONTH:

- Choose a date and time
- Interview your celebrant and book them in
- Find your venue and book that in

MONTH 2: LET'S TALK ABOUT FOOD, CAKES & SOME LEGAL STUFF

Are you planning a catered meal? What's your budget for that? Talking to friends, and looking on some of the wedding pages and groups, these costs vary wildly. You can start with nibbles in the range of $15-20 a head if you look around, or maybe you're looking for a massive bash and $95 a head isn't out of your range.

You might settle even for food carts… Just work out what you're chasing and what you can afford. It's important to clarify what is it you want? If you're looking for a basic sit down, how many courses?

Now here's a tip for someone who's arranged more than one gala event… Get onto groups and associations in the area and ask who they use. You may get lucky, find someone in your budget who can present exactly what you want.

I've even seen people talking about home catering and there's nothing wrong with that as an option either. Especially if you're having a backyard wedding. They can be lovely and personal.

Caterers are going to ask about dietary requirements, and while that's a pain and you won't know for some time, tell them that once you have RSVP's you'll send them a complete list. We had that organised for two weeks out from the event. Don't be afraid to ask questions and make suggestions. We asked for all gravies, sauces, creams and custards to be in separate jugs clearly named.

We also had a range of dietary requirements including vegan/vegetarian, intolerances and allergies, so it was vitally important to spell them out. I'm going to say to you, that while you should receive all the information in an email, make sure to reiterate your particular requirements in emails, print them out and keep them on file. (Just in case, later on, there is an issue of someone getting sick!)

After all, say you alerted them someone had a seafood allergy, then you find out that person had a reaction because there's an oyster based consommé on the table and no one knew! It does happen, so make sure you spell everything out in clear and simple English. Unfortunately (and it does happen) they may claim you didn't tell them, that's when you pull out your trusty file and show them exactly what you sent. (Look, it says on the third line on page three, mother-in-law has a seafood allergy so none at all on that table.)

Oh and back to Pinterest, because now you're looking for cakes. And yes, while cake tasting may be a thing, if you're doing it yourself, that may not be an option. (Or if you're living in the more rural areas...) For ourselves, while there are bakers in town, and they do a fabulous job, I have a friend who does them and for us, that personal touch was an important factor. So we asked, sent her photos, told her how many and decided on the layers.

Now, in case you missed it, I'm a traditional person and so is daughter, so three layers was essential. Two to cut and eat and one to keep for the first baptism. But this is something you need to decide yourself. Got six kids and there's no more? Excellent, you may want to use it all on the same day. There's no rules here. The days of mandatory fruit cake are long gone. (However, because the top layer is being frozen, we did, actually choose a fruit cake!!)

A big aspect of deciding on the cake is settling for what you want, what your budget is and finding someone. Get everything in writing and you'll likely be asked for a deposit up front.

One other thing. Cup Cakes (patty cakes) for weddings are a thing. If that's your kind of thing, go for it! Your day and your rules.

Are you considering a pre-nuptial agreement? If so, now is the time to have a chat with a solicitor. Same with any intention of a will to sign on your wedding day. We re-visit this a little later on.

Don't forget to apply for leave as soon as you can from work. If you can't do it now, put a calendar reminder on your phone!

JOBS FOR THE SECOND MONTH:

- Choose your caterer and start to think about those menus.
- Make a plan for the cake thinking of how many tiers, how you want it decorated and once you've decided that, get those quotes!
- Legal advice for a pre-nuptial agreement or will
- Apply for leave from work or set a calendar reminder for yourself.

MONTH 3: PHOTOGRAPHERS, VIDEOGRAPHERS, MUSICIANS AND MORE

In the third month let's go find ourselves some more of the essential services.

Are you going to have a videographer? A photographer? Both?

As with all the other major decisions, get online. Get quotes and check portfolios, talk to others and get their impressions. Our photographer on our wedding day was great, but it was a long time ago and we had to push to get the proofs and negatives. These days, it's a little more simple.

We chose locally again, someone who'd done gala photos for us and the bride and groom liked and were comfortable with. They settled for one photographer, (though there was an option for a second) and a package that had the photos on an online gallery. Yes, it would be behind a password, but then people could choose their own photos and arrange the printing.

For us, this was a perfect outcome. The quality of

the photos would allow for life-size portraits if they wanted. Even better, we got an awesome price too.

Now, I was talking to someone recently who was moaning about the price of a photographer and I'll tell you what I told them. "You don't go to the doctor then bitch about the price of them saving your life. Photographers are like doctors, we want their professional skills." Sure, I'm not saying you need to pay over the nose for what you want, but remember you do get what you pay for.

Again, too, be prepared the cost of a photographer may well be dependant on your location. It has been my experience if you're on the coast you may pay anything up to 3 times what you pay in a regional/rural location. So that's definitely something to look at.

Also, dependant on the location you may also have to pay up for catering for them, travelling costs and so on. Read that contract CAREFULLY before you sign on the dotted line, and if you have questions, ask them before you sign and get their answers in black and white.

I'm going to tell you to do the same with any videographer as you do with your photographer.

Now, expect to get a questionnaire asking you a million questions. The good thing is, you have time to do that. (No, don't leave it to the week before, but this is where, as the planning unfolds, you'll be able to fill in the blanks!)

Musician? DJ? Band? Don't tell me! Uncle Barry has a band and you just have to have them? Okay, again set those ground rules. What do you want? Salsa music? The latest dance craze or a quartet? Do you want them to be your Master of Ceremonies? (You can usually pay them to fill this role but check before taking this for granted.)

It's your wedding, so think about it. Some even just make up a Spotify play list. These days, you're only limited by your imagination and maybe the wobbly nature of the internet, depending on your location.

Among the ultimate questions at this juncture are, what you want to walk in to, walk out to. Will you have a father-daughter dance? What about that first dance?

Lists are great for this. And while on the subject of lists, be clear which songs you don't want played or themes of songs so you aren't surprised on the day.

We chose a local musician we know well, who's worked for us in the past and sent her a list of the 'must have music' for the reception. As to the rest, it will be easy listening and possibly even her own single.

Having said that, we also took into account the people who will be there, the ones that want to dance, and those who'll simply tap their feet.

A benefit for us, was using her sound equipment too for speeches (but don't get too excited about those until about a month or so out!)

As with everything, get it in writing. Trust me, a file is a godsend!

One other aspect I haven't talked about here, yet is the colours. Have you got your colour scheme yet? Trust me, as we get into the heavy planning work, having this nutted out now, makes so much sense!

JOBS FOR THE THIRD MONTH:

- Find your photographer and lock them in, but only after you've read the contact and are sure you understand it.
- Pay any deposit.
- Find your videographer and lock them in, but only after you've read the contact and are sure you understand it.
- Pay any deposit.
- Get your musicians/DJ on side. Ask for a contract and pay any deposit.
- Get your colour scheme organised.

MONTH 4: CARS, WEDDING PARTY AND FLOWERS

Now is an excellent time to begin thinking about how you're getting to the venue.

Horse drawn carriage in what is traditionally a wet period? In a tractor bucket on farm? Luxury stretch limo? Pick your jam, then get onto finding someone who can accomodate your needs. If you've a party of fifteen bridesmaids, two flower girls and a page boy and they and the father of the groom need a ride, I'm going to tell you, one limo is not enough!

But all jokes aside, you've now got a lot of moving parts, so think hard. You need someone reliable, responsible and if you're like me, you know someone who knows someone!

Again, looking at our experience, the father of the bride has a fully restored veteran vehicle and our bride wanted that car and Daddy to drive her. Thankfully, we also have a friend who has a similar (though different coloured vehicle) and he made himself and his car available. (They were on the guest list anyhow!)

Don't be afraid to ask friends if they have something, in most cases they'll be beyond excited to assist.

As with anything, if you're outsourcing this, get everything in writing, a contract which clearly states what they are doing, how many they can transport and their insurance. And while we're on the same note, how is the father of the bride and the mother getting home if you use a transport service?

Pro Tip: we organised a 30 seater bus, which means we were delivered to our front gate, and allowed for anyone who's had a few to also get to town safely.

Now is also the time to pick your bridal party. You'll need their assistance if you're going DIY!

Sure ask your best friend, but if they're scatty, disorganised and so on, be sure to have others you can rely on ready to jump in!

There's scads of options, from best woman and best dog through to none. Google ideas to work out what works for you best and make sure you agree on the plan.

Also, begin thinking about your Master of Ceremonies (unless you've got your DJ filling this role!) Remember, they need to be witty, funny and able to use their booming voice to get everyone's attention. They will also need a detailed timetable (we get into that next month.)

Are you having a bar? Start thinking about the drinks. Now, that may have been part of the package for catering or your venue, but if not, what drinks will you serve? Are you a dry wedding with no alcohol? A full open bar with $6 000 down for drinks?

You can consider wrist bands for over (or under 18's) so those serving know who can have alcohol at a glance. Or maybe you're only opening the bar for the bridal party. Be explicit in what you expect of the bar staff.

What about the toasts? Will you want French champagne? How will you cater for those who don't drink? (We had non-alcoholic options available.)

Spirits? Beer? Red wine and white? Moscato or chardonnay? Pick your poison. Remember to have water and soft drink and maybe even juices on tap for the little ones.

Do you need someone to man the bar? If you're doing that, I highly recommend you find someone with an RSA. (Responsible Service of Alcohol) Your venue may require a copy of this document for their files, and this covers you in the event that someone gets unruly.

Are you paying or is this a love job? Are you feeding them? (This then impacts your catering, remember!) If its a love job and you've got cousin Roland behind the bar, remember that RSA and get them enrolled and through it ASAP.

Now is the time to start looking at wedding flowers. You don't need to make decisions yet.

JOBS FOR THE FOURTH MONTH:

- Cars need to be booked, contacts signed and deposit paid.
- Choose the members of your wedding party.
- Think about the bar, who's manning it and do they need to be skilled up with an RSA?

MONTH 5: STARTING TO GET ORGANISED... INCLUDING INVITATIONS

Now is an excellent time to sit down and start thinking about the logistics of the day.

What time is the event?

How long before you leave is the photographer turning up?

Are you doing your own hair or getting someone else, likewise your makeup?

Have you decided on silk or real flowers? If they're real, when do they arrive? Do you need to keep them refrigerated?

Self-catering or outsourced?

When are you setting up?

I can hear you rolling your eyes and see the faint blush on your cheeks, but there's a reason I'm starting to ask. Depending on the time of your ceremony, you need to start making a timeline of when everyone is turning up, where you need to be...

Here's a look at our timetable:

Day before: Set up venue/rehearsal/final prep

Wedding day: 5.30am Up and quick shower.
6.00am Breakfast
6.30am Hairdressers
8.00am Makeup
9.30am Dressing (mum) and makeup (mum)
10.00am Dress bride/Photographer arrives
10.50am Load bride into vehicle
10.55am Mum leaves
11.00am Bride leaves with bridesmaid
11.20am Bride arrives at venue

Why do you need all this now? Well, you need to write your invitations, telling the guests what time to arrive. This will also impact when your cars and photographers arrive. Your caterers need to know what time they are serving, as does your celebrant and so much more.

Again, do you know someone, or is it your plan to buy 'off the shelf' or are you the DIY Queen when it comes to the invitations? There's millions of choices, and for us, I used a design program to create and order the printed copies. It's fast and cheap if you're so inclined. If not, you can look on Amazon or Ebay or even Etsy to find the perfect design either pre-designed or designed just for you.

Information should contain:

- Who is getting married
- When you're getting married

- Where you're getting married
- What time you're getting married
- When should they RSVP
- How to RSVP

Look online for samples of wedding invitations and you'll get lots of ideas.

Pro Tip: You may wish to make life easy and design or order RSVP cards and Thank You cards at the same time, so the design is cohesive. It may also save you a few more dollars.

One last thing, make sure if you're ordering invitations to order at least 10 more. Why? People lose them, you want a blank for your own memories, and if you are having alternates, they will need one too.

Now is also an excellent time to book your bouquet. How many you need will depend on your number of attendants. It is customary for the mother-of-the-bride and mother-of-the groom to have either a pin on or wrist corsage. Button holes for the men, and baskets for the flower girls.

Silk or real may be a choice dominated by price and location. Neither is better than the other. If you choose silk you can have them arrive early and be fully paid for, but real is traditional. However, you need to arrange for them to be delivered and on the day of the wedding for best outcome.

If you live near a flower market and are handy,

maybe you could do that yourself? If your budget is tight, this may be an option for you.

Flowers are essential, and for the bride, they are significant. What kind of bouquet are you after? Back to Pinterest while you consider the teardrop, tussie-mussie, and so on. And, of course, don't forget colour. Will the flowers be representative or will you have trailing ribbons. Do you want something that you can press or keep? An extra bouquet to throw? Are you planning floral centrepieces? Would silk flowers work better in this environment cutting down the 'on the day' hassle?

Which flowers do you think are you? The peony, rose or orchid even? These are so personal and yet make a statement. Are you a silk or real touch or real flower girl?

As with everything, that contract is important. Make sure it spells out what you're getting, the design and how much. When it will be delivered. Get it all in writing.

JOBS FOR THE FIFTH MONTH:

- Make a timetable of the wedding day
- Choose or design your invitations and order them.
- Flowers need to be ordered or purchased depending on your choice.

MONTH 6: THINKING ABOUT THE VENUE LAYOUT…

It's getting closer and now you've got to consider how you'll decorate the reception and ceremony venues. If you've got a venue that does this for you, make sure they have the items in the colours you desire. Find out what you still need to provide and it's time to start ordering or choosing.

Let's run through the list of important things to get sorted now:

<u>Ceremony venue</u>

- Carpet for you to walk down
- Seating, pews, ribbons
- Signing table (and chairs) and pen
- PA system
- Music for entrance
- Music for recessional
- Music during the signing
- Confetti
- Signage

Reception venue:

- Guest book
- Carpet for dance floor
- Seating
- Tables
- Tablecloths
- Crockery & cutlery
- Glassware
- Table for the cake
- Cake stand, knife, bags, topper and server
- Runners for the tables and centrepieces
- Napkins
- Place cards for seating
- Bonboniere
- Wishing Well
- Table decorations
- Signage for inside venue (in remembrance, wishing well and so on)
- Memorial photos
- Entering the venue music
- Father/Daughter dance music
- First dance music
- Leaving the venue music
- Bouquet to toss
- Selfie station if desired

As with anything, this can be done on a budget. For example my daughter wanted to make the memorial photo frames, so she bought frames, glitter and glue. Over about 3 weeks they were made outside on our back table. There's lots of options, so take a walk through Pinterest and gather your ideas. It's your wedding and your decision!

If you're doing all this yourself, make sure to find out from the venue how soon you can go in, and when you need to return to collect all your goodies.

Also if your outsourcing your custom made bonboniere (gifts for those attending) now is the time to order because you'll likely need a one-off to check carefully, before ordering the amount needed. Getting this sorted now helps to smooth out the costs too.

Clothing time!

You can spend a fortune on a gown, but this is such a personal thing. The first gown you might try one could feel like the one, but take a little longer, try a few more to be sure. Feel beautiful and take people you trust to assist you with this decision.

Some questions to ask:

- White or colour?
- Long or short?
- What kind of material?
- Bling, lace or plain?
- What's your venue?

A beach may not be the place for a full wedding gown (unless that's what you want) with elaborate crystal decorations. Take all these into account, before you choose.

Also set the tone for your attendants now, by choosing the colours. You may prefer a rainbow of colours, or one tone only. It's a good idea to get this done now and take your bridesmaids along on this journey. If they can't be there, send them images, because are they paying for it? If so, it's a good idea to consider something they would wear again. If not, then you have the opportunity to choose it all for them.

Pro Tip: If you're buying from overseas do not rely on your street clothes as a size indicator. Measurements are key. Check yourself and your attendants then choose the best fit size. Sure you wear an 8 most the time, but the 10 or even 12 may be the best option, especially if you're purchasing from China. A good measuring tape in hand, a pen and paper help you to make the right choice. Remember:

- Bust
- Hip
- Waist
- Height

Visit more than one boutique if you have to, or even your local opportunity shop if money is tight or you're looking for the perfect vintage gown. The rules are only the ones you make and most of these gowns have been worn for one day.

If it's second hand (and there's no stigma in this), check for tears and stains, you've time if these are present and don't pose an issue. Otherwise, if you know a great sewer, they may be able to unpick and create a custom pattern and/or recreate the outfit to your desired outcome. Just be aware this is super expensive!

Make sure to buy clothes bags to protect the garments and look for shoes, underwear (and you should have these well before your final fitting!!) that suit the clothing you've chosen. No use buying a strapless dress and buying a bra with straps…

Are you going veil? No veil? Hat? Stockings or bare legs?

Lots to think about, but above all, enjoy this shopping. These are moments to treasure.

Pro Tip: Get a photo of your gown and you in it. You need this for the next step!

Lastly, if you have a flower girl, now is a good time to get an idea of styles you like, but do not order until closer to the date. The last thing you need is to be fixing a dress that doesn't fit because they've had a growth spurt.

This is also the perfect time to talk jewellery. Are you going with something that you have a connection to? A family piece or is your plan new and glam?

Remember to think about your dress when you're deciding on your jewellery. Necklace, earrings and even bracelet if that's your thing.

We have a family set, and that's what daughter wore

in her day, the same as I did. It will be passed down to brides in the family. It's a lovely tradition, that suits us, but you should do what works for you.

And while we're on that subject, remember this rhyme?

Something old;
Something new
Something borrowed; and
Something blue?

In our family we add:

And a silver sixpence to wear in your shoe.

Now is also a good time to consider if you plan to adhere to this tradition.

Your dress is in the bag (literally) or ordered. Awesome. It's an excellent time to decide on your hairstyle. You can visit your local salon or find someone who specialises in wedding styles.

Take with you a list or even better, grab photos on your phone of what you like. Make sure to take your headpiece or veil and a photo of you in your dress. Talk with them, listen to their advice. But as with all things, don't be afraid to shop around. Once you've decided on a style, and the number of attendants, make sure to get the price, book the times and find out what you need to provide them to make it all come together. Some salon's will allow you to prepay in instalments before the big day.

If you need hair extensions (clip in or other) you have time to arrange another appointment ahead of the day to ensure you have everything in hand.

Are you doing something radical, like chopping it all off? Maybe you should try it beforehand, that way if you have regrets, you have time to do something about it all.

Also check if you need a hair treatment a day or so ahead, in our case, the instructions were to wash her hair, a very light conditioner the night before and part her hair where she prefers, so it wasn't too soft of the day to hold everything in place.

Start talking about rings, surnames and gifts for your attendants. There's no screaming hurry at this point, but it's good to get organised.

JOBS FOR THE SIXTH MONTH:

- Start deciding how you want to decorate the venues.
- Make a list and begin to order items or make them.

- Decide on music if you haven't yet discussed it
- Dress/Clothing shopping for you and your party (but not the flower girl dress/es)
- Purchase clothing bags
- Look at wedding rings and get ideas of what you want
- Think about how you want to work surnames
- Begin looking for attendants gift
- Jewellery
- Old, new, borrowed and blue…
- Order bonboniere
- Order/print invitations if you haven't yet

MONTH 7: TAKE A BREAK AND DO SOMETHING FUN, NEXT MONTH IS THE START OF THE MANIC PERIOD

Take a break, a holiday. Read a book. Give yourself and your fiance a break from substantive wedding planning. This is more of a cross country than a sprint!

However, it's also a good time to start on your facial regime if you haven't already.

Life's about to get really busy and you're going to begin receiving information, emails and phone calls.

Input what you have into a spreadsheet or a notebook. Keep track of payments.

Breathe!

MONTH 8: ONLY SEVEN MONTHS LEFT!

Tin tacks time.

Hens party? Bucks party? Let someone else organise them for you, but remember to have ground rules that you can live with.

If ladies of ill repute are a deal breaker, **make sure everyone knows that. Be obvious.** I know that sounds awful, but many a slip 'twixt cup and lip took place at a party like this. The bride and groom need to agree what is acceptable, allowable and what isn't. Remember, this is the template for your marriage.

Set the dates, choose the venues, then leave your party to arrange the rest. You've other things to do.

Invitations:

It's time to finalise your list of who you want to invite. You have the venue size, you know numbers and how that will impact your catering and your bar.

Whether or not there is alcohol, make a plan. Be clear with each other about who is important to you when divvying up attendance.

If parents are paying, it's considered good manners to let them have a say too, but remember, this is your day and if someone they *simply must have* is a deal breaker for you, then say no.

Get those invitations written out and addressed. You don't have to send them yet, but having them done, you can breathe easier. This is also a good time to go get postage stamps in books of 10 or 20 as needed. Remember, spread those costs around.

Make sure your invitations have a clear RSVP date.

I find a spreadsheet assists here, and I highlight when the invites go out, change the colour depending on acceptance/decline.

If you have alternates, it will make it easy for you to see how many you can include.

I also include a pre-addressed envelope with an RSVP card so people don't put the wrong address on their acceptance. I used my work PO Box for this because our mail can be a little variable, but your home address is fine, or even email if that's your choice. Make it as simple as you can for you and your guests!

By now, things should be arriving, and you'll likely be on first name basis with the parcel delivery person.

Organisation as things begin to arrive is key. I like

boxes with the names of what is in them to keep things straight. So one for venue flowers (silk for us) lighting, mirrors and jar lights.

Another for the bouquets.

One for the cake items including topper (and yes, this is the time to organise that) along with cake stand, knife and server. Bags.

Another for the flower confetti (biodegradable for us, but check with your venue.) You can make a statement depending on the flowers. We went with rosemary, rose, lavender and peonies. If you want to know more about that, google the language of flowers. We also ordered paper cones and stands.

Tealights for the pedestals and candelabra for the front of the ceremony venue were in another box. Less was best where we were holding the wedding.

Anyway, you get the idea. Boxes keep things together.

Photos talk time allowed us to navigate what we felt was important. Photos of the bride dressing (that was a no for us) but a family prayer, jewellery the bride will wear. The rings and gowns on hangers. Talk with your photographer and they will make suggestions around what they usually do. They will also likely have a checklist, or you can sniff around google and Pinterest to find one that suits your needs best.

The cars, the bride and her father before getting into the vehicle.

At the venue down the aisle, are you doing anything unusual? First kiss behind a fan or parasol? Was the groom break dancing while waiting for the bride to march down the aisle... Perhaps you parents are walking you down the aisle or even your kids? Consider what will look great and discuss with each other and the person taking your photos.

Make a list of the important dances because you want those on record too, but don't forget to also give them to your musician, DJ or make that Spotify playlist and clearly note the ones that you want at special times. (If it's a Spotify list, make sure to clue in your Master of Ceremonies so they are aware!)

JOBS FOR THE EIGHTH MONTH:

- Hens and Bucks planning, but remember to lay down ground rules.
- Write the invitations
- Think about the photos
- Make room for items arriving
- Keep your lists
- Keep paying off the wedding bills

MONTH 9: STILL LOTS TO DO

This month is all jobs related and quick!
<u>JOBS FOR THE NINTH MONTH:</u>

- Finalise the catering choosing your menu, and how you want it served.
- Your celebrant will be knocking on your door soon, because the paperwork begins to get pressing. If you don't have the right identification, now is the time to get onto it.
- Honeymoon? Plan and book now. Remember travel insurance! Research where you're going and get any travel injections planned.
- This is also the time to consider birth control if you haven't previously.
- Finalise your gift registry!
- Mail the invitations if you haven't already
- Keep paying those bills
- Keep an eye on dress size… Don't put on weight or slim down too much.

- Book your dress fitting for about 2 months before your wedding.

MONTH 10: THE DOWNHILL RUN HAS BEGUN

The invitations are out, and RSVP's should begin to dribble in. I like the shoebox style of organisation. It's on my desk as as acceptances and declines arrive, I add them to my spreadsheet and pop them in the box. They do make an interesting talking piece in twenty or thirty years!

Start wearing in the shoes around the house so they fit comfortably on the wedding day. This also tells you if you need slide in padding, and think about issues like grass. Are you likely to sink in heels? Do you need rubber caps for protection?

And while on the matter of shoes, start to prepare the wedding day grab bag. Pads, tissues, pain relief, a travel sewing kit with safety pins. Closer to the day (after your makeup trial) add lipstick in the colour you're wearing and also pressed powder for touching up during the day.

If you're the dancing queen of your group, you could consider a pair of ballet flats for later in the evening to give your feet a break.

Are you waltzing? Is now the time for dance classes? If so, get in and get them done. Now, not everyone will waltz and that's okay. If you plan to giggle and sway (we did that all those years ago then followed up with the time warp) that's perfectly okay. It's your day.

Purchase your underwear. Doesn't matter what it is, or what you like, once you book that final dress fitting, you'll need them. It's also a good time to purchase your goodies for the wedding night.

I'll leave that up to you to decide what you like or want.

Finalise your cake. Choose the flavours, number or tiers and decoration. Order the cake topper now! Make sure to get the cake maker booked, contract signed and any deposit paid (if you haven't already) and make sure you have made arrangements if necessary for a gluten free choice… or mini cake if that is easier for you and your guests.

Groom and his attendants, if you haven't yet finalised your clothes, it's time to stop procrastinating. Colours? Suit or nice pants and vest? Tie?

Who do you want matching? Is the groom in one colour and everyone else another? I highly recommend getting onto that now.

It's also time to order the gifts from Bride to Groom, Groom to Bride and your wedding party.

JOBS FOR MONTH TEN:

- Keep track of RSVP's
- Wear shoes around the house
- Prepare the wedding grab bag
- Underwear and wedding night shopping
- Finalise your cake booking
- Groom and his party shopping for clothes
- Present shopping

MONTH 11: WE'RE GOING TO THE CHAPEL IN A FEW MONTHS...

Rings.

The ultimate symbol of marriage, and it's time to get them ordered. Depending on the style of your engagement ring, you may need something specialised. Talk to the jeweller about what is best. They will make suggestions for something that won't damage your engagement ring but will be comfortable and best fit.

If you have a platinum engagement ring, then you're going to have to have a platinum wedding ring and so on. Be guided by jewellers and to be honest, it's something that's worth spending good money on, cause you're going to be wearing it for your whole life. Try more than one jeweller before settling on a ring.

Keep track of the RSVP's and remember to check in with those attending for dietary issues. Keep a list, you'll be sending it to the caterer before the big day.

Your timelines should be pretty much set in stone now, so go over it, share it with your party, MC, family and so on, so they know exactly when and how they will be needed.

This is also the time to plan for the honeymoon, thinking about clothes and passports. But if you need one and haven't yet got it sorted, do so NOW! It's also a good time to visit the smart traveller website if you're going overseas and register where you'll be.

Make sure to have a list of where and when and give it to someone you trust. (Not someone who'll drink-ring you the first night of your super romantic honeymoon!)

Make sure your celebrant has your identification sorted. In Queensland they need that no less than one month prior to complete the Notice of Intention to Marry.

Also, consider having a will ready to sign on the day. (Discuss with your solicitor.) What other things will change? Address? Names? Start making a list of these things so you can attend to them when you return from the honeymoon. Check with your state and territory to see what can be changed within a set timeframe after your wedding for free. You should have begun this planning earlier on in the planning stages.

Planning on tanning before the day? Now is the best time for a trial. This way if it doesn't work, there's time to do something about it. If you love it, great. Book your date for about a week before the wedding but at the latest 2-3 days before. Talk to your salon about what they need you to do for preparation.

JOBS FOR THE ELEVENTH MONTH:

- Purchase your rings.
- Track your RSVP's and dietary requirements list
- Share the wedding timeframes
- Honeymoon, passports and shopping
- Paperwork in order, including ID's
- Lists of name changes needed after wedding

MONTH 12: FITTINGS, FINAL INSTRUCTIONS AND FILLING OUT QUESTIONNAIRES

Time to get into that fitting! The dress fitting is a perfect time to also order the flower girl dresses. You should now have most of the payments done for the wedding itself, so you can enjoy this event.

It's also a fabulous time to hold hens and bucks parties (yes, early I know, but you'll be seriously thankful once they're over.) Think of them as the precursor to the big event.

This is also the time to book your makeup practice, nails and any health/dental needs ahead of the event.

Your last RSVP's should be dribbling in and soon, that will close. I always recommend allowing yourself 6-8 weeks because people will not return them (a small amount) and you'll need to chase them up. What it does do, is also gives you time to invite your alternates if you have spots open up due to declines.

Touch base too with all your providers, map out

how you want to set up your decorations. Finalise your music if you haven't yet.

Look after skin and body. Don't lose too much weight now and eat healthy.

This is also the time to fill out any questionnaires from your celebrant. These are important for them to 'personalise' your day. I'm also going to suggest you get these in as soon as you can. Celebrants are busy and may not be in the position to chase you up, besides, it's your day. Take that initiative.

Make sure to have one night a week (and no more) for wedding chat with your groom… It shouldn't overwhelm your life even though it's super important. Remember, at the heart of it, you're still just a boy and a girl… (or a girl and a girl or a boy and a boy…)

JOBS FOR THE TWELTH MONTH:

- Dress fitting
- Purchase flower girl dress if needed
- Hens and Bucks now!
- Hair, nails, makeup trials
- Medical and dental appointments
- RSVP's
- Finalise music
- Focus on skin and weight
- Don't get overwhelmed!

MONTH 13: A LAST BREAK BEFORE IT ALL HAPPENS!

Time to take a break. Yes, there's lots to do, but now is a good time to sit back and enjoy the ride.

JOBS FOR THE THIRTEENTH MONTH:

- Continue with the RSVP's and dietary requirements

MONTH 14: NEARLY THERE!

Right. Now is the time to chase up the missing RSVP's and arranging alternates if needed.

You should have the flower girl dress in hand now. Make clear any expectations at this point of all attendants. When you need them where, and hang any dresses and gowns to allow any creases to fall out. If needed, a careful steam a few days before may be necessary.

Now is the time to check you have any last minute issues ironed out including chasing up last minute booking with providers.

Start to set up your table seating layouts. Will you be printing them for on the door of the venue? Who will be making sure no-one (guests) rearranges them before you get inside the reception venue. (Yes, this is a thing.) And on that subject, now is the time to plan the set up of the venue. Who will be there and what time to assist with this aspect of wedding organisation?

Who and when will deliver boutonnieres for the

groom, father of the groom, and his party and the corsage for his mother?

Vows need to be written now too if you're not having a traditional wedding service. There's lots of YouTube videos and tutorials online and your celebrant may even send you some examples. Also make sure your Notice of Intention to Marry is completed and lodged.

Check you've paid the last of your vendors. Most will have a last day for payment on either contract or invoice. Once again, this is where a list assists.

Have you finalised time off as required for work, booked nails, hair and makeup for the day?

Is there a rehearsal beforehand and if so when and where? A meal afterwards?

Finish putting all your items into boxes to make your life simple and to assist with delivering to the venue the day before.

Purchase your pressed powder and lipstick ahead of time and choose your perfume! Pack your grab bag and give it to someone you trust to care for it. You'll need it after the ceremony.

One last thing… Have you got your guest book? This is a beautiful reminder of one of the most treasured days of your life. Don't leave it to the last minute!

JOBS FOR THE FOURTEENTH MONTH:

- Finalise RSVPs and contact alternates.
- Flowergirl dress should be purchased
- Hang all dresses to allow creases to fall out

- Chase up providers to ensure everything is smooth sailing
- Ensure all providers are paid in full now
- Finalise table seating charts and print out if required
- Write your vows
- Delivery of florals for groom, his family and attendants need to be settled
- Notice of Intention to Marry must be submitted
- Rehearsal booked/Dinner if necessary too
- Book nail, makeup and hair if you haven't already for the day
- Organise the last of your decorations in boxes
- Purchase pressed powder, lipstick and perfume
- Pack your grab bag
- Don't forget your guest book

MONTH 15: THE LAST WEEKS

F**our weeks out:**
The last of your planning calls should be made now. Send your caterer the final numbers and dietary requirements list.

Check in with cake vendor to make sure they're on track and when they'll deliver (or you pick up.)

Talk with your photographer about the final list of photos

Is your music picked and either sent to the musician or DJ? If not, do this now.

When will your cars arrive and do you need ribbons or will they already be on?

Has everyone who needs to give a toast been informed? Make sure to check in and see how they're going. Traditionally the toasts include:

- The Father-of the-Bride
- The Groom (and he thanks the bridesmaids for their assistance to his bride)

- The best man (responding for the bridesmaids.)

It's up to you if you choose to use those or do something different. At the end of the day, it's your wedding!

Are you having a photo site where guests can upload their photos? If so, don't forget to find a way to share the link at the event.

Three weeks out:

Vows, rings and presents. Make sure they're ready, if you haven't already, pay the last of your vendors, including your celebrant.

What are the plans for the wedding night? Is it booked and is your overnight/honeymoon bag ready? Any paperwork should now be complete.

Passports if required in hand.

Two weeks out:

Make contact with all your vendors one last time. Check and double check your plans.

Last week:

Have your bags packed. Where are you staying the

night before the wedding? (Yes I know I asked this two weeks ago, but it bears checking again.)

Are you having a girls night? If so who is in charge? When does everyone arrive? What's planned for the evening?

How are you getting to your appointments? Have you got a list of the times?

Set aside things that need to be handed over to the celebrant at the rehearsal, including any music they've requested.

Where are the rings and who will handle them until the ceremony? Have they been delivered to that person?

Send all vendors the final timing for the day.

Don't forget to give your attendants their gifts!

Hair removal... rule of thumb is undertake this several days ahead of the event, so if there's a reaction there's time to address it!

Day Before:

Are you going to the venue to set up? What time? Who's carrying everything? Who will be assisting you?

Clothes for the honeymoon are delivered to the groom.

When does the cake arrive? Who is putting it together? Also who is cutting up and distributing it? Have you told whoever which tiers can be cut and if any cannot?

Is your 'reliable person' in control of the grab bag

and anything else that needs to be taken to the venue on the day?

Give your celebrant your vows the day before, so you don't need to worry about them on the day. The less you have to take care of, the better for you.

Remind the groom to remind the best man to be on the lookout. This happened to us. I was ready and waiting and the groom didn't know I'd arrived because the best man wasn't aware we'd arrived and entered the church!

YOUR BIG DAY ARRIVES

Get up and have a quick shower (just don't get your hair wet) and have a decent breakfast. Yes, you'll have butterflies but you have a huge day ahead of you.

Brush those teeth and remember to wear a shirt which buttons up. You'll thank me later for this, once your hair and makeup are done and it's time to change!

Let your bridesmaid or mother-of-the-bride get you to your appointments.

Drink water to stay hydrated.

Don't stress. Remember those around you will do it for you and likely better than you, too! (Well, they will if they're anything like me!)

Before you dress, bathroom break. Once you're in your gown it gets a little more tricky. |

Have fun! Enjoy your day and remember to smile!

WHAT NEXT?

It seems to very overwhelming at times along the journey, but you will get there. Trust me, I've organised weddings, debutante balls and awards evenings among other events. Yes, there's lots to juggle, but a good spreadsheet and notes keep you sane. Remember to include copies of all emails, so you know exactly what's been done and said. What agreements have been made.

Above all, it's your day and it's up to what you want, what is important to you. Whether it's a wild bash at a nightclub, a romantic riverboat ceremony or micro-at-the-courthouse whatever you choose will be *your* right option.

I've attempted to make this as easy to follow as possible, but weddings are so very personal that some of what you'll find in here won't apply to you, so use this as a guide. I've also attempted to only use some of our examples, because, well, same! Besides which, the wedding is merely the precursor to a lifetime together and that's what's important.

You have a couple of things to consider after the event:

Printing of wedding photos and a wedding album and will you be letting others choose the photos they want? If so, how will you share access to the images>

Don't forget to change medicare, drivers license, passport, bank accounts, property paperwork and so on. (You need to talk to the appropriate government agencies to find this out and sort the changes.)

CHECKLISTS TO ASSIST

I n this chapter, you'll find some useful checklists:

Fill out this form to keep your planning organised

Vendor	Cost	Deposit	Current Owing	Paid in Full
Caterer				
Venue				
Photographer				
Cars				
Musician				
Videographer				
Florist				
Celebrant				
Cake				
Bar				
Gowns				
Mens Wear				

Wedding Party:
Matron of Honour (if you have one)
Bridesmaid 1
Bridesmaid 2
Bridesmaid 3

Flower Girl

Best Man
    Groomsman 1
    Groomsman 2
    Groomsman 3
    Page Boy

Colours chosen:

Wedding:
    Date:
    Time:
    Place:
    RSVP's by:
    How will they contact you?
    What's your budget?

CELEBRATION DECORATIONS

Make a list of the must have ideas for your decorations.
Describe in details what you want to achieve in the following locations.

Ceremony:

_____

_____

_____

_____

_____

Venue:

Now, make a list of the must have items you need to source to make this happen.

_____

_____

_____

_____

_____

Pro Tip: More is less in this space, so think long and hard!

THE MUSIC DECISIONS

Here, you get to write down the music you've decided on.

Processional
   Signing (choose at least 2)
   Recessional

At the reception, consider:
   What do you want to enter to?
   Father/Daughter Dance
   First Dance
   What do you want to leave to?

What other pieces are must haves for the reception?

TALKY, TALKY, TALK... TOASTS

Toasts.
Yes, most weddings have them. Here's some questions to ask:
Who do you want to talk?

<u>The Father of the Bride?</u>

<u>The Groom?</u>

<u>The Best Man?</u>

Are you planning to open the floor to anyone? Be super prepared if this happens because sometimes the toasts can be a little challenging!

If you're toast givers are unused to public speaking, have them write and practice before hand.